In the
Fifth World

To Barry and Sara —

Here is a peek at our world.
Thank you for always sharing
  yours with us.
  Love, Doug + Katie
          Gordon + Alice

In the Fifth World

Portrait of the Navajo Nation

adriel heisey + *kenji kawano*

FOREWORD PETERSON ZAH

Rio Nuevo Publishers
Tucson, Arizona

Cover

Josephine G. Catron and
Edward B. Anderson
(Honágháahnii Clan)
Mother and son,
W.W. II Marine Corps veteran
and Navajo Code Talker,
Window Rock, Arizona
—*Kenji Kawano*

Ship Rock, landmark
volcanic neck and dike,
New Mexico
—*Adriel Heisey*

Back cover

Painted Desert, north of
Petrified Forest National Park,
Arizona
—*Adriel Heisey*

Jefferson Canyon (Hashk'aa hadzohí/
Tsedeeshgizhnii Clans) and Sonya
Abe (Biih Bítoo'nii Clan)
W.W. II U.S. Army D-Day veteran
and granddaughter, Tuba City,
Arizona
—*Kenji Kawano*

Rio Nuevo Publishers
An imprint of Treasure Chest Books
P.O. Box 5250, Tucson, AZ 85703-0250
(520) 623-9558

ISBN 1-887896-31-7

Printed in Korea

10 9 8 7 6 5 4 3 2 1

Editor

Ronald J. Foreman

Design

Larry Lindahl,
Lindahl-Bryant Studio, Sedona

Map

Deborah Reade and
Kevin Kibsey

Additional photography

Kenji Kawano, p. 2
Ruth Kawano, p. 7
Andreas Bindorfer, p. 12

DEDICATION

FOR MY WIFE, Capt. Ruth Kawano, USAF, and daughter Sakura, for their love and encouragement.

—*Kenji Kawano*

FOR THE CHILDREN, who will decide where to go from here.

—*Adriel Heisey*

THE EARTH is our Mother.
Our skin is the same as the soil
from the Mother Earth, our
blood flows as the rivers that
flow from the mountains, and
our voices are like thunder.
The Great Spirit is inside each
of us. We are all part of Creation.

—*Peterson Zah*

C O N T E N T S

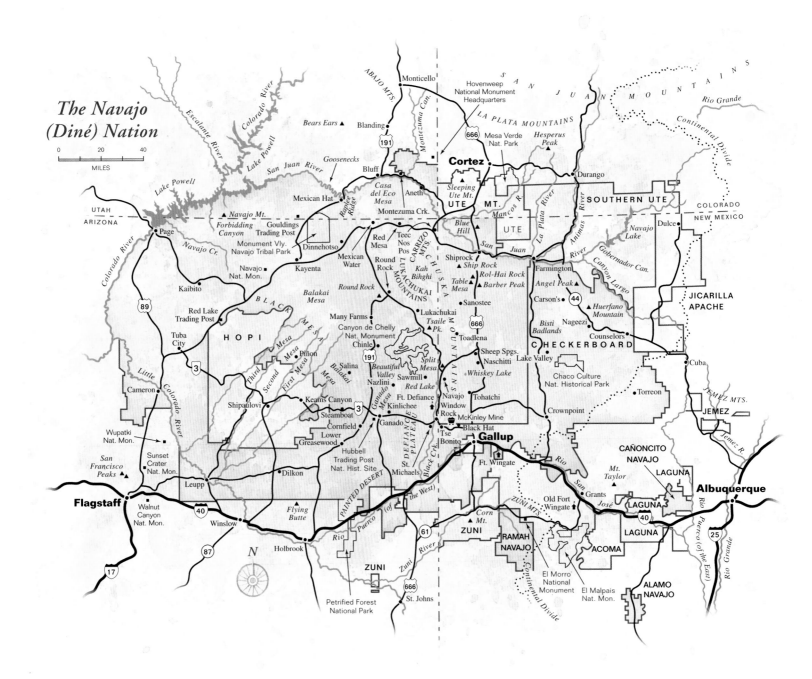

The Navajo (Diné) Nation

MILES
0   20   40

UTAH
ARIZONA

COLORADO
NEW MEXICO

Colorado River
Escalante River
Lake Powell
Lake Powell
San Juan River

Bears Ears ▲   Blanding

191

ABAJO MTS.   Monticello

Montezuma Can.

Hovenweep
National Monument
Headquarters

S A N   J U A N   M O U N T A I N S   Rio Grande

LA PLATA MOUNTAINS

Continental Divide

666   Mesa Verde
Nat. Park

Hesperus
Peak ▲

Goosenecks

Bluff

Casa
del Eco
Mesa

Aneth

Cortez   Durango

Raplee
Ridge

Sleeping
Ute Mt.

UTE   MT.

Mancos R.

SOUTHERN UTE

Mexican Hat

Montezuma Crk.

▲ Navajo Mt.
Forbidding
Canyon   Gouldings
Trading Post

Page

Navajo Cr.

Colorado River

Red
Mesa

Teec
Nos
Pos

Blue
Hill

UTE

La Plata River

San
Juan

Navajo
Lake

Dulce

Monument Vly.
Navajo Tribal Park   Dinnehotso

Mexican
Water

Round
Rock

CARRIZO MTS.

Shiprock

Farmington

Animas River

Gobernador Can.

Canyon Largo

JICARILLA
APACHE

Navajo
Nat. Mon.   Kayenta

Kah
Bihghi

Ship Rock ▲
Rol-Hai Rock ▲
Barber Peak ▲

Angel Peak ▲

Kaibito

Round Rock

Table
Mesa ▲

Carson's

44   Huerfano ▲
Mountain

Nageezi

89

Balakai
Mesa

LUKACHUKAI MOUNTAINS

Sanostee

Bisti
Badlands

Counselors

Red Lake
Trading Post

B L A C K

Many Farms

Lukachukai
Tsaile ▲
Pk.

666

Toadlena

C H E C K E R B O A R D

Tuba
City

3

HOPI

M E S A

Canyon de Chelly
Nat. Monument
Chinle

CHUSKA

Sheep Spgs.
Naschitti

Lake Valley

Cuba

Little

Pinon

191

Split
Mesa

Whiskey Lake

Chaco Culture
Nat. Historical Park

JEMEZ MTS.

Cameron

Salina

Beautiful
Valley
Nazlini

Sawmill

MOUNTAINS

Tohatchi

Torreon

JEMEZ

Colorado River

Second Mesa
Third Mesa
First Mesa

Balakai
Mesa

Red Lake

Ft. Defiance
Kinlichee

Navajo
Window
Rock

McKinley Mine

Crownpoint

Shipaulovi

Keams Canyon

3

Ganado Mesa

Tse
Bonito

Black Hat

Gallup

CAÑONCITO
NAVAJO

LAGUNA

Albuquerque

Steamboat

Cornfield

Ganado

DEFIANCE PLATEAU

St.
Michaels

Black Crk.

Ft. Wingate

Rio

Mt.
Taylor ▲

Wupatki
Nat. Mon.

Lower
Greasewood

Hubbell
Trading Post
Nat. Hist. Site

San José

LAGUNA

San
Francisco
Peaks ▲

Sunset
Crater
Nat. Mon.

Dilkon

Old Fort
Wingate

Grants

ACOMA

LAGUNA

Flagstaff

Walnut
Canyon
Nat. Mon.

Leupp

40

Flying
Butte

PAINTED DESERT

Puerco (of the West)

61

ZUNI

Corn
▲ Mt.

ZUNI MTS.

Continental Divide

40

25

Winslow

Rio

RAMAH
NAVAJO

El Morro
National
Monument

El Malpais
Nat. Mon.

ALAMO
NAVAJO

Puerco (of the East)

Rio Grande

17

N

Holbrook

Rio

Zuni River

ZUNI

666   St. Johns

Petrified Forest
National Park

87

THE NAVAJO PEOPLE—the Diné—began their great mythic journey as Insect People in the First World. When a few of these Insect People committed indiscretions that angered the Gods of the First World, all Insect People were told to "Go elsewhere, and keep on going!" Chased skyward by angry floodwaters of the First World, the people scratched at the heavens until they broke through into the Second World.

In the Second World, they encountered another group of flying creatures—the Swallow People—who agreed to ally with the Insect People to form one tribe. But in a matter of weeks, another dark incident involving an Insect Being and the wife of the Swallow People's chief again sent the Insect People into exile. As before, they punctured a hole in the sky and emerged into another world.

This Third World was the domain of the Grasshopper People. Once more, the exiles convinced their hosts to bring them in as kin. Twenty-four days later, they were again expelled for the same old transgressions. This time, Red Wind showed them the only way out, a passage through a hole it had made in the western sky.

Scouts dispatched into the bleak expanses of the Fourth World found it to be devoid of life, except for some strange creatures who irrigated fields and raised plants to eat. These beings opened their homes to the Insect Beings, and sustained them with their food. The Insect People held council and decided to mend their ways, and settle into a good life in this new place. To purify themselves in preparation for becoming fully human, the Insect People spent several days performing ablutions, or ceremonial baths. Then, one bright morning, the Holy People formed First Man and First Woman from two ears of corn.

By intermarrying with the numerous children of First Man and First Woman, the Insect People were transformed into human beings. But then came Coyote, the Trickster, who enraged the Water God of the Fourth World and precipitated another flood. This deluge swept The People and all Animal Beings skyward. Barely escaping with their lives, they all emerged in the center of a small island in a vast lake.

With the help of Black Wind, these Earth-Surface People managed to dry out a path from the island to the shore. And thus, from this tenuous foothold, the ancestors of those who would become the Navajo Nation began their ultimate journey in the Fifth World.

OUR STORIES teach us where we come from and who we are. They say we arrived here in this, the Fifth World, after dwelling in four lower worlds. These stories were originally spoken and sung, not written down, so there are many versions. We are called the Earth-Surface People because of our ancestral existence in the other worlds. We have lived in the present world for a long time, and our land abounds with places whose names allude to our legends. We made history here and, despite all the adversity, we endure. We are here to stay.

More Diné people dwell on Mother Earth than ever before. More of us speak the language and hear the stories, which make us hungry to learn more about the old ways. Yet we who take pride in our ancient skill of adapting the ways of non-Indians to our own pragmatic ends are continually challenged. With a median age of less than eighteen years, the Diné population is heavily under the influence of the dominant society, and our young people thirst for all things new. Tradition is eroding as the tides of mainstream American culture swirl around us. We cannot stop these tides, nor would it be desirable to do so even if we could.

I often speak to high school and college students, many of whom are members of other American Indian tribes. I observe that they often draw a sense of identity from their cohorts— groups we adults might call gangs. I tell them that I have my own gang, too, and I show them pictures of my traditional people back home. No matter how far I journey, I know where my roots are. It is a precious thing to know where your umbilical cord was placed. We who understand this are charged with making sure our young ones have the opportunity to learn this, too. The glitter of modern life can distract them if we do not deliver the promise of their deeper inheritance. That is why education is important. It may not solve everything, but it will solve many things.

The value of these photographs arises from this deeper inheritance. The images do not parrot the abundant clichés of

Diné life, and some will be surprising to those who know little of life on the Reservation. Kenji Kawano and Adriel Heisey have not flinched in their resolve to show us their view of the Diné world, no matter how complex and incongruous its parts may seem.

I have known these men professionally and personally for many years, and attest to their efforts with special conviction. In the course of developing their respective careers of journalism and aviation, both men have given of themselves to serve the Diné. They have lived among us, shared our community, eaten our food, witnessed and even joined in our struggles. They bring their vision to bear with affection, respect, and understanding.

It is courageous of them to present their photographs in this manner. Although their time on the Reservation overlapped by almost a decade, and they knew one another while here, their respective images were not necessarily created with a common objective in mind, and the differences in their methods and interests are obvious. However, I also see a fascinating dynamic in the juxtaposition of their work. Kenji Kawano's portraits

permit us to look into the eyes and lives of his subjects, and are informal and revealing. Adriel Heisey, on the other hand, transports us to an exalted vantage point and empowers us to see the larger landscape that both inspires and is marked by Diné lifeways. Both men bring us beauty, humility, and appreciation of People and Land.

Ours is a time when beauty and wonder often succumb to the press of existence. These photographs show us a people whose traditions hold these values in great esteem. They revitalize our own aesthetic values, and they encourage us to reflect on our place in the world. I invite you to accept and enjoy this gift.

—*Peterson Zah*
Former Chairman and President
Navajo (Diné) Nation

EARTH

k e n j i   k a w a n o

THE FIRST TIME I saw an Indian, I was six years old. My dad strapped me to the back of his bicycle and took me to the movies. I don't remember the name of the picture we saw, only that it was an American western and that I never wanted it to end.

As a Japanese boy growing up in the 1950s and 1960s, I loved westerns, particularly those directed by the great John Ford. "Stagecoach," "She Wore A Yellow Ribbon," "The Searchers," and "Cheyenne Autumn" were just a few of the movies that my dad and I saw together. Like him, I was fascinated by the magnificent landscape of the American West and the exotic Indians who resided there. I had no idea whether the Indians I saw on screen were portrayed fairly. I only knew that I identified with them, and that they and the land they inhabited seemed to be one.

The movies fueled my desire to become a photographer, and to one day visit America. In 1973, at the age of 24, I finally got the chance. I landed in Los Angeles—movie capital of the world—but quickly realized that I would not find the mythic western landscape or Indians there. To see The West, I would have to travel east.

And so, in March 1974, I boarded a Greyhound bus bound for New Mexico. I got off the bus in Gallup, and there at the station I saw my first "real" Indian. She was an elderly Navajo lady, and she had wrapped herself in a colorful woolen blanket to ward off the late winter chill.

From Gallup, I hitchhiked into the heart of the Navajo Reservation and found a job pumping gas at a service station in Ganado, Arizona. Later I worked as a janitor, maintenance man, and photographer at the College of Ganado, and it was there that I met Ruth Williams.

She was an attractive young woman with long black hair and a strong sense of style. I tried to talk with her several times, but it was hard. I was a janitor, and she was a student. I was Japanese, and she was Navajo. I couldn't speak English very well, and my Navajo was even worse.

But Ruth knew I was also a photographer, and one day she asked me: "Are you like all those other photographers who just show half truths about Navajo life, the parts that look nice and traditional?" It was the opening I needed. She listened patiently as I told her about myself, about life in Japan, and why I had come to the Navajo Reservation.

I also discovered that Ruth's brothers already knew about me. They would come from Steamboat to Ganado to fill up at the little gas station where I had first worked. Someone dubbed me the "Jumping Japanese" because I seemed over-eager to serve the customers. They were amused to see such behavior on the laid-back reservation.

Before I left Japan, I promised my parents that I would only be gone for a few months. But as my relationship with Ruth blossomed I realized that was one promise I would not be able to keep. Ruth and I were married in 1978, and the sun quickly set on any notion I ever had of returning to Japan to live. The real American West had become my home, and Indians were now family.

In 1980, I became official photographer for the Navajo Nation. As a member of then-Chairman Peter McDonald's entourage, I traveled often and widely. I had an opportunity to meet many Navajo people in communities throughout the reservation, and they got to know me. With my Japanese face, name, accent, and camera, I wasn't easy to forget.

The government job had its perks, but covering official, staged "photo ops" was not exactly an end in itself. I still longed to work as a *real* photojournalist. And so, in 1985, I accepted a position as staff photographer with *Navajo Times Today*, which had just become a daily newspaper.

When Chairman McDonald stopped the presses at *Navajo Times Today* in 1987, I suddenly had plenty of time to devote to a project that had become my passion: Creating a portrait portfolio of Navajo Code Talkers, a special group of Marine Corps veterans whose "unbreakable code," based on the Navajo language, was a best-kept secret that helped America defeat Japan in World War II. Images from this portfolio appeared in my first book, *Warriors: Navajo Code Talkers*, published in 1990.

The success of *Warriors* encouraged me to create the photographs that appear in this book. As a Japanese man who married into the Navajo world, I am acutely sensitive to the challenges Navajos face living in this, the Fifth World. The Navajo story of creation and emergence—to which the title of this book alludes—is all about change, and I especially admire how the Navajo people honor the traditions of their elders while adapting to the political, economic, and cultural realities of American life.

I wanted to capture the real warp and weft of Navajo life today while being ever mindful of my wife Ruth's admonition about avoiding "half truths." So I photographed people as I found them—at home, at work, and at play.

To reveal both the enduring values and remarkable resilience of the Navajo people, I focused on relationships between pairs of individuals. My portraits include those of husbands and wives, parents and children, brothers and sisters, and even three sets of twins. Among the Navajo people, extended families are still the rule. It is quite common to find three or more generations living under one roof, and so many of these portraits are of grandparents and grandchildren.

Perhaps my personal favorite is the portrait of Mr. Edward B. Anderson, Jr. and his 98-year-old mother, Mrs. Josephine G. Catron, which appears on the cover of this book and on page 4.

Mr. Anderson, one of the veterans featured in *Warriors*, served with the 1st Marine Division in Australia and New Guinea. When I told him I was looking for subjects to photograph for this project, he told me about his mother, who lived in Window Rock. She turned out to be one of the most charming and gracious people I met.

Mrs. Catron walked with a cane, but when I arrived with my camera she tossed her cane aside and quickly changed into a fresh outfit. I asked her if she would rather be seated for the photograph, but she preferred to stand. Her wood stove made an ideal backdrop, and the available light streaming in through the nearby widow was lovely, but in order to capture the moment I realized I would have to set up my tripod on Mrs. Catron's bed. No problem. If I had asked to *move* the bed, Mr. Anderson and I probably would have had to restrain Mrs. Catron from doing it herself.

I certainly did not expect Mrs. Catron, a Navajo lady born in the late nineteenth century, to speak English. After all, I had met many Navajo elders much younger than she who only spoke Navajo. I assumed Mr. Anderson would have to serve as our interpreter, but Mrs. Catron turned out to be far more fluent in English than I was. She told me she had learned the language as a young woman working at a reservation hospital five miles from her home. In those days, she didn't have a wagon or even a horse. So she walked to work and back, ten miles a day, for more years than she cared to remember.

When Navajo people greet one another for the first time, custom and courtesy require each to first disclose the names of the clans to which their parents belong. Navajo society is matriarchal, and so the identity of the mother's clan takes precedence over the father's, and together they reveal more about an individual's family background than a surname alone. I wanted to honor this tradition by including in the captions as much clan information as my subjects were willing to share with me. A full list of Navajo clan names and their English translations appears at the end of this book.

I could not have achieved the sense of emotional depth and intimacy I was after with this project without first earning the consent and trust of the people I photographed. And so, to everyone who graciously helped me create a more honest, respectful portrait of Navajo people today, I say *ahe'hee* and hope you and your families will find this work worthy of your trust. ■

S K Y

a d r i e l   h e i s e y

I FIRST VISITED NAVAJOLAND when I was 20 years old.
I had taken a semester's leave from professional pilot training
to accompany a friend who had signed up to student teach
at a Bureau of Indian Affairs boarding school on the Navajo
Reservation. As a fledgling pilot, I already had logged a couple
of hundred hours in the air, all flown in the East, and had seen
many impressive landscapes. But I was unprepared for the scene
that opened to us as we trundled down out of the San Juan
Mountains of Colorado into the proto-rural emptiness of the
Four Corners.

I struggled to make sense of this new kind of space. Far out
on the southern horizon, Ship Rock vaulted heavenward from
the primeval plains like a dark cathedral. And as we drove
further into the heart of the Navajo Nation, every new vista
invited contemplation. To me, born and raised in the lush
Cumberland Valley of Pennsylvania, this arid landscape of earth
and sky seemed mythic and monumental.

On my family's farm back home, I had built muscle and bone
in fields that laid bare the Earth's own body. Forest groves

bordered these plots of rich soil, waiting to re-clothe their
primeval domain. Farther out, the Appalachian Mountains rose
up gently to stem the sky's hazy sprawl. Years of living amid
these contours made them so familiar to me that I had only
to glance at the nuanced skyline to know where I was. I felt
connected and held.

That first fall living in Kinlichee I encountered a people who
sang night-long stories in which *their* land played a starring
role. Their horizon had places with lilting names like Lohali,
Balakai, Lukachukai, and Agathla, and they would point to these
landmarks and be certain you'd know which they meant. I soon
found myself scanning the horizon each time I came into the
open, like a child checking for the reassuring gaze of a watchful
adult. For all the vast spaces and strange shapes of this land
between the sacred mountains, I felt remarkably at peace there,
and accepted.

In 1984, after establishing my professional pilot credentials
in the East, I returned to the Navajo Nation to live and work.
Navajo people became my community and my passengers as I

took a position with the government's air transportation department. It may seem improbable that an Indian tribe would have its own fleet of airplanes, but the Navajos are the largest, most populous, and most resource-rich tribe in the United States. With so many people spread over such a large area and lots of coal in the ground, they need—and can afford—their own airplanes to do the people's business.

My job was to transport the tribe's decision makers around the country quickly and safely. Sometimes we would make a short hop to another part of the reservation in the single-engine Cessna, braving low-level turbulence and dirt airstrips dotted with sheep. To reach a distant metropolis, I would fly one of the tribe's speedy turboprop King Airs at airliner altitudes. The variety of flying was a pilot's dream.

My most frequent passengers, of course, were tribal Chairman and President Peterson Zah, his staff, and his family. His role kept him relentlessly in the limelight, and his schedule often called for him to be in several locations in one day.

Getting to know my passengers on a first-name basis was something of a fringe benefit of the job. But there could be awkward moments. One morning shortly after I hired on, Mr. Zah arrived on the tarmac to board the plane I had readied for him. Always the people person, Mr. Zah greeted me warmly as I met him at the door.

"Good morning, Tim," Mr. Zah said cheerfully. I smiled and politely explained that Tim was the *other* new pilot, and that my name was Adriel.

"Ahhhh!" he said in mock exasperation, "All you white guys look the same!"

The fact that fellow pilots and I were Anglo was good in certain respects: when political tensions in the government were simmering, non-Navajo pilots assured neutrality in the cockpit. But it could be awkward, also. When I would visit schools to talk to groups of Navajo students about my job, they would invariably ask if there were any Navajo pilots. I would explain that, aside from a few individuals who chose other vocations after flying for the military, there simply weren't any Navajos who were qualified. I always encouraged young Navajo students to consider a career in aviation so that someday they, too, could fly for the Navajo Nation. I'm happy to report that the day is fast approaching.

Years of flying out of Window Rock gave me endless opportunities to see the land in all of its various moods of season, weather, and light. Stowing a camera under my seat on every trip, I was always ready. Passengers came to know me as the photographer pilot, even though I took care to keep my priorities straight.

One summer evening I was flying Mr. and Mrs. Zah home to Window Rock from a chapter meeting in Kayenta. Monsoon storm clouds had erupted over the Chuska Mountains, far enough east of our route to allow us to enjoy the drama without threat of their violence. Sunset light raked past us to bathe the distant anvils in unearthly hues of yellow and rose. Below, purple shadows filled the Chinle Valley. With the plane on autopilot, I reached down for my camera and discreetly snapped a few frames. I knew the Zahs well enough by then to feel confident that they wouldn't mind. But as I put down my camera, I heard a muffled voice from behind. I lifted one ear cup of my headphone and turned my head back toward the cabin. It was Mrs. Zah.

"I can't believe you get paid to do this!" she repeated. She sounded so deadpan, I wasn't sure how to take her remark. I shrugged and smiled sheepishly. Mrs. Zah kept me hanging for a moment, and then broke into a hearty laugh.

Occasionally, the plane would be empty, as when I would deadhead to pick up passengers. Those legs were prime opportunities for me to shoot because I could maneuver the plane into radical attitudes in order to get clear shots straight down. I would describe these adventures to Navajo students when I showed them slides I had made this way, and these usually were the images that garnered the most interest. Their eyes would widen with wonder as my photographs allowed them to see their homeland in a new way. After one such presentation to Jill Farkas' photography class at Tse Ho Tso Middle School in Fort Defiance, I received a letter from a particularly enthusiastic young woman.

"I think you are very daring to do the things you do to get the pictures," she wrote. "But they are all worth it. There is one question I would like to ask since I didn't have time yesterday:

if you see a very good picture and just have to have it, but you also have passengers in the plane, would you warn your passengers and risk scaring them to death to get the picture?"

My answer was "No, of course not!" But she had hit on the central problem: making pictures was always at the bottom of my task list as Navajo Nation pilot. And so, in order to pursue my photography muse, I decided to build my own airplane in my spare time while I continued to fly for the Nation. The plane I constructed, a Kolb Twinstar, is so slow and open that I can take pictures straight down simply by leaning over the edge of my seat while the wings stay level. Its sole purpose is to serve as a platform for photography, the results of which are evidenced in this book.

My plane folds quickly and fits in a trailer I tow with my truck. This enables me to take pictures in distant locations without having to fly there. On a typical shoot for this project, I would drive out from Window Rock to a promising area I had scouted on a previous, "official" flight. With a couple of days to spend, I could set up a little campsite at the turnoff to a well or stock tank along a flat stretch of dirt road that would serve as a makeshift runway. My operation would make quite a spectacle out on the lonely range.

If (as often happened) a family drove by and slowed down to stare, I'd wave them in for a closer look. Their standard question, "What are you doing here?" would get my standard reply, "I take pictures from my plane because this land is so beautiful."

And I'd invite the curious, especially the kids, to sit in the pilot's seat. After that, we would generally be on the same wavelength. More than once, conversations around the open cockpit of my airplane would steer me toward a new point of interest on that textured horizon the locals knew so well.

I built my plane so that the camera pod can be removed easily and replaced with a passenger seat. Sometimes, when conditions were just right, I'd offer a ride. Word of these flights got around, and neighborhood children would come racing to the airport on their bicycles, armed with permission notes from their parents, whenever they spied my plane in the sky over Window Rock. Over the years, I gave dozens of kids their first glimpse of home from above. The intercom usually stayed quiet during these flights, save for my terse commentary on what we were seeing.

But judging from the expressions on their faces, I would say my young passengers were invariably spellbound.

It was a singular pleasure to live and work among the Navajo people. I was an ethnic minority in their midst, sometimes the only Anglo around. Nevertheless, I felt accepted and appreciated in a way that belies the tribe's painful history with outsiders. Perhaps my sense of belonging lay in a fortuitous intersection of my own shyness with the characteristic Navajo reticence— a tendency to avert the eyes out of respect, a gentle handshake, a healthy regard for personal space, a tolerance for silence. I also have an affinity for the Navajo reverence for the great natural system in which all our lives are held.

During my years working for the Navajo Nation, I learned a great deal from passengers, colleagues, friends, and teachers. Through them, I came to understand that the Navajo people regard the entire landscape as sacred, and that the Holy People travel the sky to keep watch over the land and its inhabitants.

The sky is where I work, and the land and people are what I see. The Navajo people helped me recognize that my aerial vantage point is a privileged one. I am both delighted and humbled to share the fruits of that privilege, especially with the people who dwell between the sacred mountains. ■

In the
Fifth World

◀ Pow wow dancers
at Navajo Nation Fair,
Window Rock, Arizona
▶ Yé'ii Bicheii ceremony
at the base of the
Carrizo Mountains,
west of Teec Nos Pos,
Arizona

◄ LaTonya Williams (left) and Octavia Williams
(Todich'íí'nii/Náneeshłézhi Táchii'nii Clans),
sisters, Steamboat, Arizona
▲ Native American Church meeting,
Lukachukai, Arizona

▲ Cherlyn Williams (Tséníjíkiní/Náneeshłézhi Táchii'nii Clans)
(left) and Martika Williams (Tábaahi/Náneeshłézhi Táchii'nii
Clans), cousins, Steamboat, Arizona
▶ Tepees attract tourists at I-40 travel stop, Gallup, New Mexico

◀ LeAnn Holiday and Rochelle Holiday (Táchii'nii/Tó'aheedliinii Clans),
twins at Navajo Song and Dance Contest, Window Rock, Arizona

▲ Darleen Hardy and Marleen Hardy, sisters, Shiprock, New Mexico

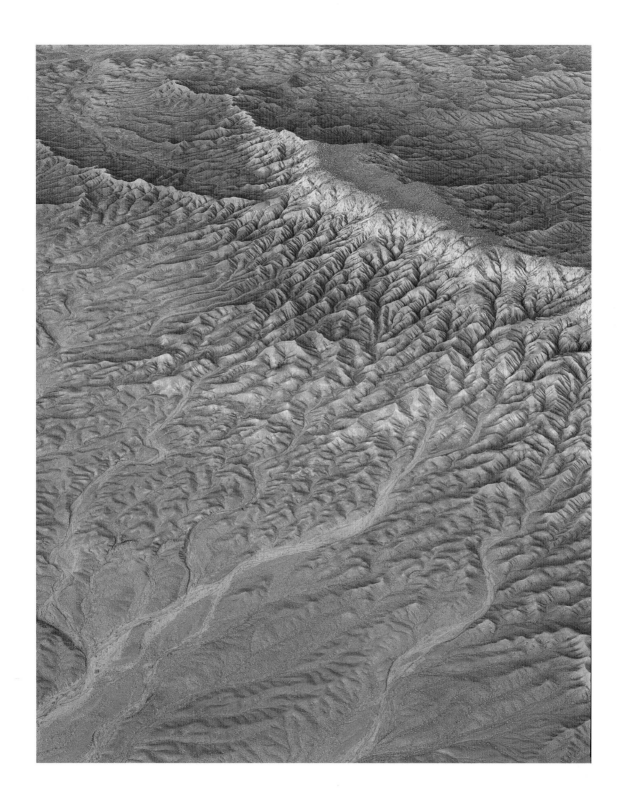

◀ Painted Desert, north of Petrified Forest National Park, Arizona

▶ Jefferson Canyon (Hashk'aa hadzohí/Tsedeeshgizhnii Clans) and Sonya Abe (Biih Bítoo'nii Clan), W.W. II U.S. Army D-Day veteran and granddaughter, Tuba City, Arizona

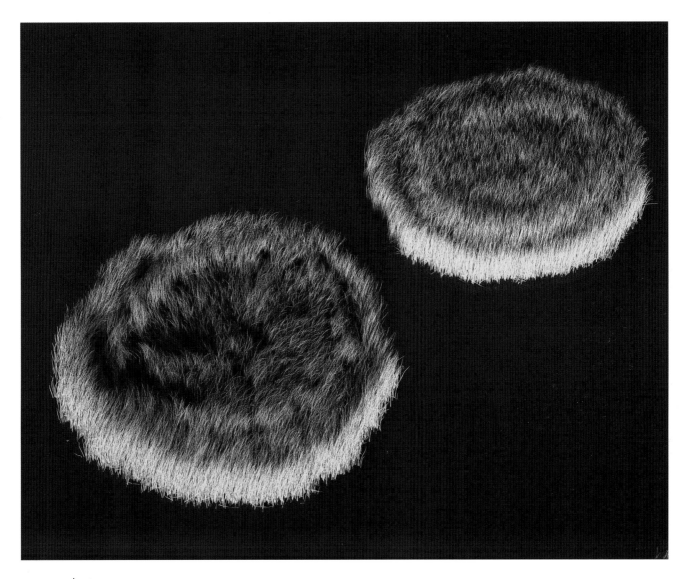

◄ Cedric Williams (left) and Galen Williams

(Todich'íí'nii / Náneeshłézhi Táchii'nii Clans),

brothers, Steamboat, Arizona

▲ Grass hummocks in Red Lake, north of Navajo, New Mexico

▲ Nathaniel Cisco (front) (Kinyaa'aanii / Ashiihi Clans)
and Ervin Yazzie (Biih Dine'é / Kinyaa'aanii Clans)
Cousins, Canyon de Chelly, Arizona
▶ Autumn-gold cottonwood trees line the San Juan River
near Bluff, Utah

◀ Dirt road through sagebrush, Ganado Mesa, Arizona

▶ Derrick Williams (Tabłłhí/Náneeshłézhi Táchii'nii Clans) and Galen Williams (Todich'íí'nii/Náneeshłézhi Táchii'nii Clans), cousins, Steamboat, Arizona

◄ Agnes Yoe
(Honághááhnii Clan)
(left) and Alice Howard
(Todich'íí'nii Clan),
friends, Dilkon, Arizona
► Saturday parade,
Navajo Nation Fair,
Window Rock, Arizona

◄ Navajo Nation Fair,
Window Rock, Arizona
▶ Ryan West (left)
and Renee West
(Kinyaa'aanii/Táchii'nii
Clans), brother and sister,
Window Rock, Arizona

◀ Moonrise over Gallup, New Mexico

▲ Tom Fannie (Naakaii Dine'é Clan)

and Cody Dayish, father and son,

Shiprock, New Mexico

◀ Cordell Segay (left)
and Aaron Segay
(Naakaii Dine'é Clan),
brothers,
Sawmill, Arizona
▶ Indian rodeo at
Navajo Nation Fair,
Window Rock,
Arizona

38

▲ Ben Lee, Jr. (left) and Nathaniel Lee
(Kinyaa'aanii/Biih Bítoo'nii Clans),
brothers, Window Rock, Arizona
▶ Jeremiah Thompson (left) and Joshua
Thompson (Táchii'nii/Tsi'naajínii Clans),
twins, Fort Defiance, Arizona

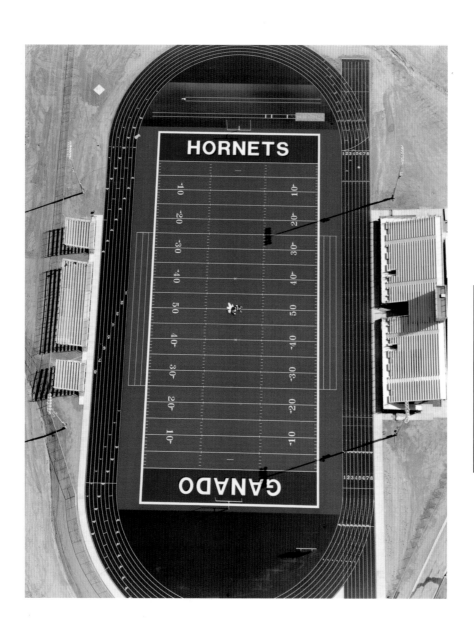

◀ New artificial turf
at Hornets Stadium,
Ganado High School,
Ganado, Arizona
▶ Ronald Tsinnie
(Haltsooí Dine'é Clan)
(front) and Jason
Manuelito, teammates,
Tohatchi High School,
Tohatchi, New Mexico

▲ Andrea Beyal (left) and Audrey Beyal
(Todich'íí'nii / Kinyaa'aani Clans), twins,
Fort Defiance, Arizona
▶ Cul-de-sacs, Fort Defiance, Arizona

45

◀ West Mitten,
Monument Valley Navajo
Tribal Park, Arizona-Utah
▶ Chinle Creek, Canyon
de Chelly National
Monument, Arizona

◀ Jimison J. Ben, Jr.,
(Deeshchii'nii / Todich'íi'nii
Clans) and Jimmie Joe Ben
(Todich'íi'nii Clan),
W.W. II Navy veteran
and grandson,
Crownpoint, Arizona
▶ Alice Roanhorse
(Tsenahabiłnii / Bit'ahnii
Clans) and Krystal Begaye
(Tsenahabiłnii / Tł'iziłani
Clans), weaver and
granddaughter,
Fort Defiance, Arizona

48

◀ Charlene Leuppe
(Todich'íí'nii/
Deeshchii'nii Clans)
and Karen Leuppe
(Todich'íí'nii/
Táchii'nii Clans),
aunt and niece,
Miss Navajo Nation
1994-1995,
Kinlichee, Arizona
▶ Sharon Watson,
Miss Navajo Nation
1991-1992, above
Window Rock,
Arizona

◄ Navajo Nation Council
Chambers, Window Rock,
Arizona

▶ Martin Enfield (left)
(Táchii'nii/Tsi'naajínii Clans)
and Dwayne Clauschee
(Kinyaa'aanii Clan),
friends, Diné College,
Tsaile, Arizona

▲ William Draper (Ashiihi/Tó'aheedliinii Clans) and
Matthew Garret Draper (Naakaii Dine'é/Táchii'nii Clans),
school principal and grandson, Nazlini, Arizona
▶ Ganado Primary School, Ganado, Arizona

54

▲ Todilto Park, northeast of Navajo, New Mexico

▶ Donald M. Johns (left) and Joe Reed (Naakaii Dine'é Clan), brothers and shepherds, St. Michaels, Arizona

◀ Summer sheep camp, near
Whiskey Lake, New Mexico
▶ Laura Johnson Nez
(Hashtł'isbnii/Táchii'nii Clans)
and Vernon Francis Nez
(Dził tł'ahnii/Tótsóhnii Clans),
newlyweds, Sawmill, Arizona

58

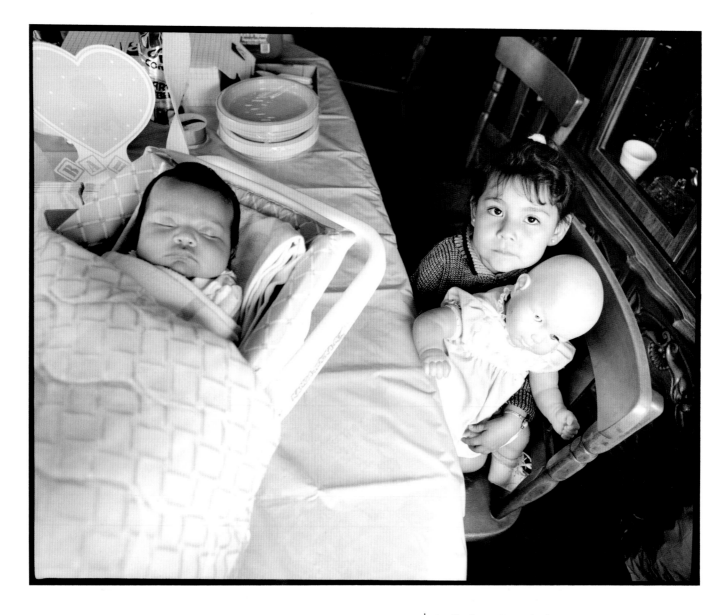

▲ Cherlyn Williams (left) and Sondra Williams
(Tsénįíkiní/Náneeshłézhi Táchii'nii Clans), sisters,
Steamboat, Arizona

▶ Mobile home on freshly graded site,
Tse Bonito, New Mexico

◀ Pigeon Springs
housing development,
Fort Defiance, Arizona
▶ Edward C. Cadman
(Kinyaa'aani Clan) and
Edward C. Cadman II
(Kinłichíí'nii Clan),
Navajo Police Officer and
son, Nazlini, Arizona

▲ Fresh feed for the flock, Window Rock, Arizona

▶ Randy Nolan Smallcanyon and Sherry Dyana Nez

(Tábaahí Clan), brother and sister, St. Michaels, Arizona

▲ "Muttonman" cartoonist Vincent Craig (Tł'ógí)
and Dustin Craig (Butterfly [Apache]/Tł'ógí Clans),
father and son, Window Rock, Arizona

▶ Sheep grazing near Flying Butte, a volcanic cone,
north of Holbrook, Arizona

◀ Dragline exposes
coal seams at
McKinley Mine,
Black Hat,
New Mexico
▶ Chevrons on
Raplee Ridge,
San Juan River
near Mexican Hat,
Utah

◄ Sheep grazing near Stoney Buttes, Lake Valley, New Mexico

▲ Leonard Begay (Deeshchii'nii / Kinyaa'aanii Clans) and
Helen Bighouse (Deeshchii'nii / Todich'íi'nii Clans), grandson
and grandmother, Large Dry Lake, Arizona

◀ Gabriel Benally
and Emmett Chischilly
(Tl'aashchi'í Clan),
son and father,
Fort Defiance, Arizona
▶ Cornfield in
Beautiful Valley,
north of Nazlini,
Arizona

◀ Earthen sweat
lodge with smoke hole
and east-facing door
at foot of Balakai Mesa
near Salina, Arizona
▶ Archielly Chischilly
(Tl'aashchi'í/
Todich'íi'nii Clans)
and Benson Johnson
(Tótsóhnii/Tábaahí
Clans), father and son
preparing for sweat
lodge ceremony,
Fort Defiance, Arizona

▲ Jerome James (Táchii'nii Clan) and Edgar James (Táchii'nii/Todich'íi'nii Clans), son and Vietnam War Army veteran father, Navajo, New Mexico

▶ Sheep return to Split Mesa corral at sunset, north of Navajo, New Mexico

◀ Summer sheep camp
in winter, Chuska
Mountains north of
Toadlena, New Mexico
▶ Wilber Smith (left)
(Náneeshłézhi Táchii'nii/
Honágháahnii Clans)
and Thomas Smith
(Honágháahnii/
Todich'íi'nii Clans).
son and father,
Yé'ii Bicheii Dancers,
Cornfield, Arizona

◀ LaTonya Williams (left) and Galen Williams
(Tsénijíkiní / Náneeshłézhi Táchii'nii Clans),
sister and brother, Steamboat, Arizona

▲ Hogan with Christmas lights, Fort Defiance, Arizona

▲ Roofless house along Black Creek,
near Navajo, New Mexico
▶ Irene Bahe (left) and Nellie Rose
(Tl'iziłani/Kinyaa'aanii Clans), sisters,
Black Mesa, Arizona

▲ Yesbah Tsosie (Táchii'nii/Yoo'í Dine'é Clans)
and Erickson Tim Preston (Táchii'nii/Tótsóhnii Clans),
great great grandmother and great great grandson,
Many Farms, Arizona
▶ Huerfano Mountain (Dził na'oodiłii), legendary home
of First Man, First Woman, and Changing Woman,
southeast of Bloomfield, New Mexico

CLAN NAMES

NAVAJO (DINÉ)	ENGLISH
Ats'osi Dine'é	Feather People
Ashiihi	Salt Clan
Ashiinii (extinct)	Salt People
Azee'tsoh Dine'é	Big Medicine People
Beiyóodzíne' Dine'é	Paiute People
Bííh Dine'é	Deer People
Bííh Dine'é Táchii'nii	Deer People of Táchii'nii
Biih Bítoo'nii	Deer Spring Clan
Biihtsoh Dine'é	Big Deer People
Biihyázhí Dine'é	Little Deer People
Bít'ahnii	Folded Arms People
Bit'aanii (extinct)	Talks-In-Blanket Clan
Chíshí	Chiricahua Apache
Deeshchii'nii	Start-Of-The-Red-Streaked People
Dibé łizhiní	Black Sheep—San Felipe Clan
Dichin Dine'é	Hunger People

Diłzéehi	Mohave Clan
Dólii Dine'é	Blue Bird People
Dzaanééz łání	Many Mules (Burros) Clan
Dził Ná'oodiłnii	Turning (Encircled) Mountain People
Dził t'aadnii	Near the Mountain Clan
Dził tł'ahnii	Mountain Cove Clan
Gah Dine'é Táchii'nii	Rabbit People of Táchii'nii
Halgai Dine'é	People of the Valley
Haltsooí Dine'é	Meadow People
Hashk'aa hadzohí	Yucca Fruit-Strung-Out-In-A-Line Clan
Hashtł'ishnii	Mud Clan
Honágháahnii	One-Walk-Around Clan
Hooghan łání	Many Hogans Clan
'Iich'ah Dine'é (extinct)	Moth People
Jaa'yaalóolii Dine'é	Sticking-Up-Ears People
K'aa' Dine'é	Arrow People
Keha'atiinii	Foot-Trails People
Kinłichíí'nii	Red House People—Zia Clan
Kinlitsonii	Yellow House People
Kinyaa'áanii	Towering House People
Lók'aa' Dine'é	Reed People
Ma'iitó	Coyote Spring People
Ma'iideeshgiizhinii	Coyote Pass People—Jemez Clan
Naadáá Dine'é	Corn People
Naakétł'ahí	Flatfoot People—Pima Clan
Naałani Dine'é	Many Commanche Warriors Clan
Naakaii Dine'é	Mexican Clan
Naashashí Dine'é	Bear Enemies—Tewa Clan

Naashgalí Dine'é	Mescalero Apache Clan
Naasht'ézhí Dine'é	Zuni Clan
Naayízí Dine'é	Squash People
Naayíziłtsooi Dine'é	Pumpkin People
Náneesht'ézhí Táchii'nii	Charcoal-Streaked Division of Táchii'nii
Nát'oh Dine'é	Tobacco People
Níhoobáanii	Gray-Streak-Ends Clan
Nóóda'i Dine'é	Ute Clan
Nóóda'í Dine'é Táchii'nii	Ute Division of Táchii'nii
Sei Bse Hooghnaii	Sand Hogan People
Taadiin Dine'é	Corn Pollen People
Tábaahí	Water's Edge Clan
Táchii'nii	Red-Running-Into-The-Water Clan
Ta'néészahnii	Badlands People
Tł'ógí	Weavers—Zia Clan
Téeatiin	Trail-To-Garden People
Ti'izhiłizhíní Dine'é	Black Goat People
Tazhii Dine'é	Turkey People
T'iisch'ebaanii	Gray-Cottonwood-Extend-Out People
Tl'aashchí'í	Red Cheek People
Tl'iziłani	Many Goats Clan
Tó'áhaní	Near-To-Water Clan
Tó'aheedliinii	Water-Flows-Together Clan
To'azoli	Light-Water People
Tóbaazhní'ázhí	Two-Who-Came-To-Water Clan
Tódích'íi'nii	Bitter Water Clan
Tódík'ozhí	Salt Water Clan
Tótsóhnii	Big Water Clan

Ts'ah Yísk'ídnii	Sagebrush Hill Clan
Tsédeeshgizhnii	Rock Gap Clan
Tséghadínídinii	Crystal Rock
Tsenahabiłnii	Sleep-Rock (Over-Hanging Rock) People
Tséníjíkiní	Cliff Dwelling Clan
Tseíkeehé	Two-Rocks-Sit Clan
Tsetaa'aanii	Rock-Extends-Into-Water People
Tseyanatohnii (extinct)	Horizontal-Water-Under-Cliffs People
Tsezhindii'aai	Slanted-Lava-Spire People
Tsi'naajínii	Black-Streaked-Wood People
Tsín Síkaadnii	Clamp Tree Clan
Tsin Yee Na'alo'ii Dine'é	Tree Stretcher People
Yé'ii Dine'é	Giant People
Yoo'í Dine'é	Bead People

T O O L S

ADRIEL HEISEY

Cameras and Lenses

Canon EOS 620 (35mm)

20-35mm, 35-135mm, 75-300mm

Pentax 67 and 645N

45mm, 55mm, 75mm, 90mm,

135mm, 165mm, 200mm, 300mm

Film

Fujichrome 100, 400

Kodak Lumiere 100

Kodachrome 64, 200

Gyrostabilizer

Kenyon KS-6

Aircraft

Kolb Twinstar

specially modified for aerial photography

KENJI KAWANO

Camera and Lenses

Pentax 67

55mm, 75mm, 90mm, 200mm

Film

Kodak T-MAX 400

Print Paper

Oriental Seagull VC-FB

Variable Contrast D.W. Glossy